MW00442552

Table of Contents

Our Story

The Meeting Place on Market
220 West Market Street, Lima Ohio

In 2003, Ruth Ann and Greg Stover, with their daughter and son-in law, Jennifer and Kevin Brogee, opened a gourmet coffee shop and café in downtown Lima, Ohio. Designed as a community gathering place, as well as purveyor of their premium KaffeeScape® brand coffee, it was named The Meeting Place on Market. At that time, Mary Weis, independent baker, delivered mouth-watering desserts on a regular schedule. After a few years, Mary was able to devote more and more of her time in baking for The Meeting Place on Market, becoming their head baker. Soon after, Mary proposed creating gluten-free baked goods as an additional option. Jennifer quickly agreed, especially since she had discovered a gluten-free diet was of benefit to her son, who struggled with hyperactivity at school. Relying on her years of baking experience, and absorbing as much information from others as she could, Mary fine-tuned her recipes, creating healthy, great tasting gluten-free food from whole ingredients. She also started teaching others how to successfully cook and bake with gluten-free cooking classes at the café. Her cooking class attendees encouraged her to share her expertise with others through a cookbook. This easy to follow cookbook is the result of her success!

All recipes in the cookbook are gluten-free. For the sake of simplicity, we have not labeled the recipes using the word "gluten-free"; gluten-free is assumed.

Enjoy!

Mary Weis teaching her gluten-free cooking class

Dedication

This cook book is dedicated to Eloise Buettner, mother of Mary Weis, and long-time baker at home for her family. For the past number of years she spent many hours baking alongside her daughter for The Meeting Place on Market. Eloise brightened any room she walked into with her smile and positive spirit and she is sorely missed.

Eloise Buettner

Gluten-Free Basics

With these 6 basic recipes, you can convert many of your favorite "gluten-filled" recipes into gluten-free!

Homemade Gluten-Free Noodles

Brown Rice Flour Mix

Ingredients:

2 cups brown rice flour

⅓ cup tapioca starch (or tapioca flour)

⅔ cup potato starch

Instructions:

Mix very well. Store in an air tight container and use within a month. Can be stored in the freezer to extend the freshness longer than 1 month.

Mary's Tip: Because I use large amounts of this mix, I double or triple the recipe when I mix it.

White Rice Flour Mix

Ingredients:

2 cups white rice flour

⅓ cup tapioca starch (or tapioca flour)

⅔ cup potato starch

1 Tbsp. xanthan gum

Instructions:

Mix very well. Store in an air tight container and use within a month. Can be stored in the freezer to extend the freshness longer than 1 month.

Mary's Tip: Because I use large amounts of this mix, I double or triple the recipe when I mix it.

Cream of Mushroom Soup

Ingredients:

4 Tbsp. butter

2 Tbsp. slightly heaping arrowroot

2 cups chicken stock, warm

2 cups heavy whipping cream

½ tsp. salt

⅛ tsp. pepper

¼ cup fresh mushrooms, chopped small

Instructions:

1. Melt butter in large saucepan over low heat.

2. In a separate bowl, whisk together warm chicken stock with arrowroot, salt, pepper, and whipping cream. Mix well, then continue stirring as you add the melted butter.

3. Increase heat and bring mixture to a slight boil, stirring constantly. Turn heat to medium-low. Soup should be thickened and a creamy mixture.

4. Add mushrooms, stir until mushrooms are hot. Serve immediately or freeze for use in recipes.

Croutons

Ingredients:

½ loaf of stale Gluten-Free Better Bread (see recipe page 40)

4 Tbsp. butter

2 Tbsp. olive oil

½ tsp. garlic powder

½ tsp. onion powder

½ tsp. dried oregano

½ tsp. dried basil

Pinch of salt

Instructions:

1. Preheat oven to 350°. Slice bread and remove crusts. Cut into small squares of crouton size.

2. On 2 large cookie sheets melt butter and combine the rest of the ingredients together.

3. Mix the melted butter with the bread squares and distribute across both cookie sheets.

4. Bake in oven at 350°, stirring every 10 minutes until crunchy.

5. Remove from oven and leave out to cool.

Bread Crumbs

Use a stale loaf of Gluten-Free Better Bread (see recipe page 40) and set it out to dry for about 5 days. Break into small pieces and blend in a blender until the consistency of coarse bread crumbs. Store in an air-tight container.

Homemade Noodles

Ingredients:

1 dozen eggs

1 Tbsp. xanthan gum

2 tsp. salt

Brown rice flour

Tapioca starch

Instructions:

1. Beat eggs, xanthan gum and salt.

2. For every cup of rice flour, add approximately ⅓ cup of tapioca starch. Keep adding flour to egg mixture until dough starts to stiffen.

3. Pour out onto a very well-floured cloth and roll into a log.

4. Cut into chunks and make into balls. Take each ball and roll out on flour surface until thin.

5. Put on upside down cookie sheet and place in oven at 250° for a few minutes until they feel dry, but not over dry.

6. Take out and cut into strips.

7. Spread out on fabric table-cloth for 2-3 days, until completely dry, or bag and put into freezer.

Cookies & Moon Pies

Chocolate Marshmallow Moon Pies

Thumbprint Cookies

Ingredients:

1/3 cup oil

½ cup sugar

1 1/4 cups brown rice flour

2 eggs

1/4 tsp. baking soda

1 tsp. baking powder

1/2 tsp. salt

1 1/4 tsp. xanthan gum

1 tsp. vanilla

Topping Ingredients:

3/4 cup pecans, finely chopped

1/2 cup jam or icing

Instructions:

1. Preheat oven to 350°. Lightly grease a cookie sheet.

2. In a medium-sized bowl, beat oil and sugar together.

3. Add the rest of the dry ingredients and mix well.

4. Using a teaspoon, create balls of dough – one for each cookie. Roll each ball in the pecans until coated.

5. Place ball on cookie pan. Press cookie to 1/3 inch thickness. Press center of cookie with thumb to create a small well in the center of the cookie dough.

6. Bake for 10 minutes, until lightly browned.

7. Let cool. Fill cookie indentations with jam or filling of choice.

Sugar Cookies

Ingredients:

¾ cup butter

1 cup sugar

1 egg

1 Tbsp. vanilla

2 cups Brown Rice Flour Mix (see recipe page 7)

1 tsp. baking powder

1 tsp. xanthan gum

¼ tsp. salt

Instructions:

1. Beat butter, sugar, egg and vanilla until creamy. Add flours until dough is formed.

2. Wrap in plastic wrap or wax paper and refrigerate for 30 minutes.

3. Roll into log. Cut ¼ inch slices and lay flat on cookie sheet.

4. Baked at 350° for 12-15 minutes.

5. Decorate with your choice of icing and/or sprinkles.

Chocolate Chip Cookies

Dry ingredients:

½ cup brown rice flour

½ cup tapioca flour

¼ cup potato starch

½ tsp. baking soda

1 tsp. xanthan gum

¼ tsp. salt

Wet ingredients:

¼ cup shortening

¾ cup brown sugar

1 egg

5 Tbsp. sugar

2 tsp. vanilla

1 cup chocolate chips

1 Tbsp. water

Instructions:

1. Blend dry ingredients.

2. Add wet ingredients and stir until blended.

3. For each cookie, use two teaspoons to shape ball of dough. Drop onto a well-greased cookie sheet, allowing a couple inches between each cookie.

4. Bake for 9 minutes at 350°.

Peanut Butter Cookies

Wet ingredients:

1 cup shortening

1 cup peanut butter

1 cup sugar

3 eggs

2 tsp. vanilla

Dry ingredients:

3 cup brown rice flour

1 tsp. baking powder

1 ½ tsp. baking soda

½ tsp. salt

Instructions:

1. Cream together shortening, peanut butter and sugar. Add eggs and vanilla and mix until blended.

2. In separate bowl, mix dry ingredients.

3. Add dry ingredients to wet ingredients and mix well.

4. Drop by teaspoon onto cookie sheet. Use fork tines to press down center of each ball of cookie dough, making imprint.

5. Bake at 350° for 9-10 minutes, or until centers begin to set.

Chocolate Marshmallow Moon Pies

Ingredients:

⅓ cup shortening

½ cup sugar

1 ½ cup brown rice flour

1 egg

½ tsp. salt

½ cup plain yogurt

¼ tsp. baking soda

2 tsp. baking powder

1 tsp. xanthan gum

½ tsp. vanilla extract

Filling:

Marshmallow cream

Glaze:

1 cup semi-sweet chocolate chips

2 Tbsp. shortening

Instructions:

1. Preheat oven to 350°. In a medium sized bowl, combine the shortening and sugar. Beat well with mixer on medium.

2. Add the brown rice flour and beat well until smooth. Scrape the sides of the bowl at least once during mixing.

3. Add the remaining batter ingredients and mix well, until the dough comes together. The dough will be soft but manageable.

4. Press dough to 1/8 inch thickness and cut with a 2 inch circle cutter. Place slices on sprayed pan. OR, use moon pie pan and fill with dough.

5. Bake for 9-10 minutes at 350° degrees, until edges are slightly browned. Remove from oven and cool on wire racks.

6. For filling, spoon a heaping teaspoon of marshmallow cream on half of the moon pie, and top with the other half.

7. For glaze, combine the chocolate chips and shortening in a microwave safe bowl. Cook in microwave on high for about 1 minute or so, until melted. Stir. (Can also melt in sauce pan on low heat over burner, stirring until melted).

8. To assemble cookies, place marshmallow cream between 2 cookies and cover completely with chocolate. Place on wax paper to set.

9. Makes 6-8 moon pies.

Red Velvet Moon Pies

Ingredients:

⅓ cup vegetable oil

½ cup sugar

1 cup brown rice flour

1 Tbsp. unsweetened cocoa powder

1 egg

½ cup plain yogurt

1 tsp. baking soda

½ tsp. salt

¾ tsp. xanthan gum

1 tsp. vanilla extract

1 tsp. red food coloring

Filling:

⅓ cup shortening

¾ cup confectioner's (powdered) sugar

4 oz. cream cheese

½ tsp. vanilla extract

Instructions:

1. Preheat oven to 350°. In a medium sized bowl, combine the oil and sugar. Beat well with mixer on medium.

2. Add the brown rice flour and beat well until smooth. Scrape the sides of the bowl at least once during mixing.

3. Add the remaining batter ingredients and mix well. The dough will be thick like cake batter.

4. Drop rounded tablespoonful's of dough onto the sprayed pan. Cookies will spread slightly during baking.

5. Bake for 9-10 minutes at 350° degrees, until the cookies take on a bit of color on the edges and the tops appear dry and springy to the touch. Let cool on racks.

6. For filling, blend all ingredients using electric mixer on medium, until light and fluffy.

7. To assemble cookies, place a tablespoon of filling between 2 cookies and press together to form a sandwich. Place on wax paper to set.

8. Makes 6 moon pies.

Chocolate Moon Pies

Ingredients:

⅓ cup vegetable oil

½ cup plain yogurt

¾ cup sugar

1 tsp. baking soda

1 cup brown rice flour

½ tsp. salt

⅓ cup unsweetened cocoa powder

½ tsp. xanthan gum

1 egg

1 tsp. vanilla extract

Filling:

⅓ cup shortening

4 oz. cream cheese

¾ cup confectioner's (powdered) sugar

½ tsp. vanilla extract

Instructions:

1. Preheat oven to 350°. In a medium sized bowl, combine the oil and sugar. Beat well with mixer on medium.

2. Add the brown rice flour and beat well until smooth. Scrape the sides of the bowl at least once during mixing.

3. Add the remaining batter ingredients and mix well. The dough will be thick like cake batter.

4. Drop rounded tablespoonful's of dough onto the sprayed pan. Cookies will spread slightly during baking.

5. Bake for 9-10 minutes at 350° degrees, until edges are slightly browned and the tops are slightly springy. Remove from oven and cool on wire racks.

6. For filling, blend all ingredients using electric mixer on medium, until light and fluffy.

7. To assemble cookies, place a tablespoon of filling between 2 cookies and press together to form a sandwich. Place on wax paper to set.

8. Makes 6-8 moon pies.

Oatmeal Crème Moon Pies

Ingredients:

½ Tbsp. raisins

1 ¼ cup rolled oats (gluten-free)

⅓ cup vegetable oil

¾ cup brown sugar

1 egg

½ tsp. salt

½ tsp. xanthan gum

1 tsp. vanilla extract

1 Tbsp. water

Filling:

⅓ cup shortening

¾ cup Confectioner's (powdered) sugar

½ cup marshmallow cream

Instructions:

1. Preheat oven to 350°. Finely mince raisins (combining a little bit of oats with the raisins will make this easier). Place the raisins and oats into a blender. Process until most of the oats are powdery, yet a good amount of small pieces remain.

2. Pour the oat mixture into large mixing bowl. Add the remaining batter ingredients and mix well. A sticky looking dough will form.

3. Place tablespoonfuls of dough on the sprayed cookie sheet and use moistened fingertips to press down to ¼ inch thick.

4. Bake for 8-10 minutes at 350° degrees, until edges are slightly browned. Remove from oven and let the cookies rest on pan for a couple of minutes before transferring to cooling rack.

5. For filling, combine shortening and Confectioner's sugar using electric mixer on medium, until creamy. Add the marshmallow cream and mix well.

6. To assemble cookies, spread filling on bottoms of cookies and press together with second cookie to form a sandwich. Place on wax paper to set.

7. Makes 6 moon pies.

Orange Biscotti

Ingredients:

2 cups Brown Rice Flour Mix
(see page 7)

1 cup sugar

1 ¼ tsp. baking powder

1 Tbsp. orange peel

1 tsp. xanthan gum

2 eggs

3 Tbsp. water

1 ½ tsp. vanilla extract

1 ½ tsp. orange extract

Instructions:

1. Preheat oven to 350°. Grease 2 cookie sheets.

2. Mix dry ingredients in mixing bowl. Add eggs, water, and extracts. Mix with wooden spoon until well blended.

3. Divide dough into two evenly sized balls. Press each ball onto a cookie sheet. Use hands to form a log about 4 ½ inches wide and about 11 inches long. Ensure the log is the same thickness from end to end. Bake for 40 minutes at 350°.

4. Remove from oven. Cut diagonal strips about ½ inch to ¾ inch wide. Place each strip on its side and bake 15 minutes.

5. Remove from oven and turn each piece onto opposite side and bake another 15 minutes.

6. Remove from oven and drizzle with melted chocolate. (Melt gluten-free chocolate bark in microwave until of drizzling consistency. Drizzle using a fork.)

7. Let icing dry completely before bagging or wrapping.

Peppermint Biscotti

Ingredients:

2 cups Brown Rice Flour Mix (see recipe page 7)

1 cup sugar

1 ¼ tsp. baking powder

1 tsp. xanthan gum

2 eggs

3 Tbsp. water

1 ½ tsp. vanilla extract

1 ½ tsp. peppermint extract

Instructions:

1. Preheat oven to 350°. Grease 2 cookie sheets.

2. Mix dry ingredients in mixing bowl. Add eggs, water, and extracts. Mix until well blended.

3. Divide dough into two evenly sized balls. Press each ball onto a cookie sheet. Use hands to form a log about 4 ½ inches wide and about 11 inches long. Ensure the log is the same thickness from end to end. Bake for 40 minutes at 350°.

4. Remove from oven. Cut diagonal strips about ½ inch to ¾ inch wide. Place each strip on its side and bake 15 minutes.

5. Remove from oven and turn each piece onto opposite side and bake another 15 minutes.

6. Remove from oven and drizzle with melted white chocolate. (Melt gluten-free white chocolate bark in microwave until of drizzling consistency. Drizzle using a fork.)

7. Let icing dry completely before bagging or wrapping.

Mary's Tip: Add red food color, or other desired colors, to the icing.

Chocolate Biscotti

Ingredients:

1 ½ cups Brown Rice Flour Mix (see recipe page 7)

1 cup sugar

1 ¼ tsp. baking powder

½ cup cocoa powder

1 tsp. xanthan gum

2 eggs

3 Tbsp. water

3 tsp. vanilla extract

Instructions:

1. Preheat oven to 350°. Grease 2 cookie sheets.

2. Mix dry ingredients in mixing bowl. Add eggs, water, and vanilla. Mix with wooden spoon until well blended.

3. Divide dough into two evenly sized balls. Press each ball onto a cookie sheet. Use hands to form a log about 4 ½ inches wide and about 11 inches long. Ensure the log is the same thickness from end to end. Bake for 40 minutes at 350°.

4. Remove from oven. Cut diagonal strips about ½ inch to ¾ inch wide. Place each strip on its side and bake 15 minutes.

5. Remove from oven and turn each piece onto opposite side and bake another 15 minutes.

6. Remove from oven and drizzle with melted white chocolate. (Melt gluten-free white chocolate bark in microwave until of drizzling consistency. Drizzle using a fork.)

7. Let icing dry completely before bagging or wrapping.

Tip: Add red food color, or other desired colors, to the icing.

Cranberry Almond Biscotti

Ingredients:

2 cups Brown Rice Flour Mix (see recipe page 7)

1 cup sugar

1 ¼ tsp. baking powder

1 tsp. xanthan gum

2 eggs

3 Tbsp. water

1 ½ tsp. vanilla extract

1 ½ tsp. almond extract

¾ cup crushed almonds

½ cup dried cranberries

Instructions:

1. Preheat oven to 350°. Grease 2 cookie sheets.

2. Mix dry ingredients in mixing bowl. Add eggs, water, and extracts. Mix with wooden spoon until well blended. Add almonds and dried cranberries and mix well.

3. Divide dough into two evenly sized balls. Press each ball onto a cookie sheet. Use hands to form a log about 4 ½ inches wide and about 11 inches long. Ensure the log is the same thickness from end to end. Bake for 40 minutes at 350°.

4. Remove from oven. Cut diagonal strips about ½ inch to ¾ inch wide. Place each strip on its side and bake 15 minutes.

5. Remove from oven and turn each piece onto opposite side and bake another 15 minutes.

6. Remove from oven and drizzle with melted white chocolate. (Melt gluten-free white chocolate bark in microwave until of drizzling consistency. Drizzle using a fork.)

7. Let icing dry completely before bagging or wrapping.

Fudge Macaroons

Ingredients:

½ cup evaporated milk

¾ cup sugar

2 Tbsp. butter

1 tsp. vanilla

1 ½ cup chocolate chips, or ¾ cup chocolate chips plus ¾ cup butterscotch chips

2 cups gluten-free corn flakes (unfrosted)

1 ½ cups flaked coconut

½ cup nuts, chopped

Instructions:

1. Combine milk, sugar and butter in saucepan until reaches low boil. Boil for about 2 minutes, stirring constantly. Remove from heat.

2. Add vanilla and chocolate/ butterscotch chips. Mix well.

3. Add corn flakes, coconut and nuts, stir until coated with chocolate.

4. Use two teaspoons to form ball and drop onto wax paper, evenly spaced.

5. Let cool until hardened.

Desserts & Pies

Brownies

Brownies

Ingredients:

1 cup shortening

⅔ cup cocoa

2 cups sugar

4 eggs, beaten well

2 tsp. vanilla

¼ cup water

1 ½ cup brown rice flour

4 tsp. baking powder

1 cup nuts (optional)

Instructions:

1. On low heat, melt the shortening in a saucepan.

2. Add cocoa and sugar and stir until blended. Remove from heat.

3. Add the beaten eggs, vanilla and water, stir.

4. In small bowl, mix the brown rice flour, baking powder and nuts (optional). Add to the wet mixture and stir until smooth.

5. Pour into greased 9x9 inch square pan. Bake for 15-20 minutes at 350° F.

Vanilla Cake

Ingredients:

1 ½ cup sugar	1 Tbsp. baking powder
½ cup butter	½ tsp. xanthan gum
4 eggs	¾ cup milk
2 cup brown rice flour	2 tsp. vanilla extract
½ tsp. salt	

Instructions:

1. Preheat oven to at 350° F. Choose either two round pans or one 9x13 oblong pan. Line bottoms of pans with parchment paper or wax paper. Grease pans with cooking spray.

2. Beat butter and sugar in mixing bowl until light and fluffy. Add eggs and beat well. Scrape bowl, mix. Add rest of ingredients and beat for about 1 minute.

3. Pour batter into pans and bake for about 25 minutes at 350° F, or until toothpick comes out clean.

4. If using oblong pan, cool completely, then frost with your favorite frosting. If using round pans, let cool for about 10 minutes and remove from pan, then remove wax paper from bottom of cake. Let cool completely and frost cake, putting a layer of frosting in between layers. Ice sides, top and decorate.

Mary's Tip: Can be used to make cupcakes too!

Carrot Cake

Ingredients:

3 cups brown rice flour	2 cups sugar
1 ½ tsp. xanthan gum	1 ½ cups vegetable oil
1 Tbsp. baking powder	4 large eggs
2 tsp. baking soda	2 tsp. vanilla extract
1 tsp. salt	2 cups grated carrots
2 tsp. cinnamon	1 cup walnuts
½ tsp. nutmeg	1 cup shredded coconut

Cream cheese icing:

½ cup butter (softened)	3 cups powdered sugar
½ cup cream cheese (softened)	1 tsp. vanilla extract

Instructions:

1. Preheat oven to 350° F. Spray a 9x13 rectangular pan with cooking spray.

2. Beat sugar, oil and eggs in mixing bowl until smooth. Add vanilla and mix well.

3. Add dry ingredients to mixing bowl and mix with electric mixer for 1 minute, until smooth and well-mixed. Fold in carrots, walnuts, and coconut.

4. Pour batter into pan and bake approximately 20-25 minutes. Check for doneness with a toothpick.

5. To make icing, blend all ingredients together thoroughly.

6. Let cake cool completely, then frost with icing.

Mary's Tip: Carrot cake is best baked in an oblong pan. This cake is slightly crumbly and tends to crack or break when moving it.

Pie Crust

Ingredients:

1 cup white rice flour

1 Tbsp. sugar

½ tsp. salt

¼ tsp. baking powder

⅓ cup shortening

½ tsp. vanilla extract

⅓ cup cold water

Instructions:

1. Mix all ingredients except water together until crumbly.

2. Start adding very cold water, slowly, until dough starts to form a ball.

3. Place dough into pie pan and press out evenly.

4. If dough is too thick, remove some until you reach desired thickness.

5. This crust can be pre-baked for a cream pie, or filled with filling for a fruit pie.

Apple Pie

Ingredients:

5 cups sliced tart apples

1 cup sugar

1 tsp. cinnamon

⅛ tsp. nutmeg

½ tsp. salt

3 Tbsp. cornstarch

Gluten-Free Pie Crust (see recipe page 31)

Oatmeal topping:

1 cup gluten-free oatmeal

¼ cup butter

5 Tbsp. sugar

2 Tbsp. white rice flour

Instructions:

1. Preheat oven to 350° F.

2. Mix all of the ingredients in a glass bowl and microwave on high for 10 minutes. Remove from microwave and stir well. Return to microwave and cook another 7 minutes. Stir well. Apples should be starting to thicken. (Or, combine in sauce pan on stove. Heat over medium heat, stirring constantly, until thickened.)

3. Pour into gluten-free pie crust.

4. Prepare oatmeal topping by mixing topping ingredients until crumbly.

5. Cover top of pie with oatmeal topping and bake at 350° F for about an hour, or until bubbly.

Blackberry Pie

Ingredients:

5 cups blackberries

¾ cup sugar

4 Tbsp. cornstarch

Gluten-Free Pie Crust (see recipe page 31)

Oatmeal topping:

1 cup gluten-free oatmeal

¼ cup butter

5 Tbsp. sugar

2 Tbsp. white rice flour

Instructions:

1. Preheat oven to 350° F.

2. Mix berries, sugar and cornstarch together.

3. Pour into gluten-free pie crust.

4. Prepare oatmeal topping by mixing topping ingredients until crumbly.

5. Cover top of pie with oatmeal topping and bake at 350° F for about an hour, or until bubbly.

Rhubarb Pie

Ingredients:

5 cups rhubarb

1 ⅓ cup sugar

4 Tbsp. cornstarch

Gluten-Free Pie Crust (see recipe page 31)

Oatmeal topping:

1 cup gluten-free oatmeal

¼ cup butter

5 Tbsp. sugar

2 Tbsp. white rice flour

Instructions:

1. Preheat oven to 350° F.

2. Mix rhubarb, sugar and cornstarch together.

3. Pour into gluten-free pie crust.

4. Prepare oatmeal topping by mixing topping ingredients until crumbly.

5. Cover top with oatmeal topping and bake at 350° F for about an hour, or until bubbly.

Cherry Pie

Ingredients:

5 cups cherries

¾ cup sugar

½ tsp. cinnamon

⅛ tsp. almond extract

4 Tbsp. cornstarch

1 Tbsp. butter

Gluten-Free Pie Crust (see recipe page 31)

Oatmeal topping:

1 cup gluten-free oatmeal

¼ cup butter

5 Tbsp. sugar

2 Tbsp. white rice flour

Instructions:

1. Preheat oven to 350° F.

2. Mix cherries, sugar, cinnamon, almond extract, cornstarch and butter together in a glass bowl. Cook in microwave for 10 minutes. Stir and return to microwave for 7 minutes. Stir. (Or, combine in sauce pan on stove. Heat over medium heat, stirring constantly, until thickened.)

3. Pour into gluten-free pie crust.

4. Prepare oatmeal topping by mixing topping ingredients until crumbly.

5. Cover top with oatmeal topping and bake at 350° F for about an hour, or until bubbly.

Peanut Butter Pie

Ingredients:

Gluten-Free Pie Crust (see recipe page 31)

1 box cook & serve vanilla pudding

1 heaping Tbsp. peanut butter

¼ cup powdered sugar

Whipped topping:

1 cup whipping cream

2 Tbsp. sugar

Instructions:

1. Bake pie crust at 350° until edges are golden brown.

2. Cook pudding according to the directions on the box.

3. Mix peanut butter and powdered sugar with fork. Set aside 2 Tbsp. for topping. Crumble remaining mixture on top of baked pie crust.

4. Pour pudding into pie crust. Set aside to cool

5. Make whipped topping by combining whipping cream and sugar in a cold bowl. Use cold beaters and whip with electric beater until soft peaks form.

6. Once cool, spread whipped topping on top and sprinkle remaining peanut butter mixture on top.

Peach Pie

Ingredients:

5 cups peach

¾ cup sugar

½ tsp. cinnamon

1 tsp. lemon juice

4 Tbsp. cornstarch

1 Tbsp. butter

Gluten-Free Pie Crust (see recipe page 31)

Oatmeal topping:

1 cup gluten-free oatmeal

¼ cup butter

5 Tbsp. sugar

2 Tbsp. white rice flour

Instructions:

1. Preheat oven to 350° F.

2. Mix peaches, sugar, cinnamon, lemon juice, cornstarch and butter together in a glass bowl. Cook in microwave for 10 minutes. Stir and return to microwave for 7 minutes. Stir. (Or, combine in sauce pan on stove. Heat over medium heat, stirring constantly, until thickened.)

3. Pour into gluten-free pie crust.

4. Prepare oatmeal topping by mixing topping ingredients until crumbly.

5. Cover top with oatmeal topping and bake at 350° F for about an hour, or until bubbly.

Rice Pudding

Ingredients:

2 cups cooked rice	½ cup sugar
1 ¼ cup milk	1/8 tsp. salt
2 eggs, beaten	½ cup raisins
¼ tsp. cinnamon	½ tsp vanilla

Instructions:

1. Microwave milk for 3 minutes on high, stir.

2. Microwave milk again for 3 minutes, or until almost boiling. Stir.

3. Combine eggs, sugar and salt in a 2 quart casserole.

4. Stir in scalded milk. Mix in rice, raisins, cinnamon and vanilla thoroughly.

5. Microwave mixture 3 minutes on high, stir.

6. Microwave again 3 minutes on high, stir again.

7. Let stand 5-10 minutes until set.

Jennifer's Tip: This is pure comfort food, and is a favorite for my family on lazy Sunday evenings.

Breads & Muffins

Gluten-Free Better Bread

Gluten-Free Better Bread

Dry ingredients:

2 cups white rice flour

1 cup White Rice Flour Mix (see recipe page 7)

3 tsp. xanthan gum

1 ½ tsp. salt

2 Tbsp. sugar

Wet ingredients:

3 eggs, beaten

2 Tbsp. melted butter

1 tsp. vinegar

1 ½ c. warm water

2 Tbsp. yeast

Instructions:

1. In medium-sized bowl, combine dry ingredients.

2. In large measuring cup, add water, yeast, vinegar, and melted butter. Let set for 5 minutes.

3. Blend all ingredients well. Mix 2 to 3 minutes on medium speed.

4. Pour into a greased bread pan. Cover dough and let set for 30 minutes, until doubled in size.

5. Preheat oven to 350° F.

6. Bake in oven for 50 minutes, until lightly browned. Remove from oven and let cool.

Challah Bread

Ingredients:

2 cup white rice flour	2 tsp. sugar
1 ¾ cups tapioca flour	1 ½ Tbsp. yeast
¼ cup sugar	4 Tbsp. butter, melted
3 tsp. xanthan gum	1 cup warm water
½ tsp. salt	1 tsp. apple cider vinegar
⅔ cup warm water	4 eggs

Instructions:

1. Preheat oven to 350° F. In medium mixing bowl, blend white rice flour, tapioca flour, sugar, xanthan gum, and salt.

2. In small bowl, combine ⅔ cup warm water, sugar and yeast. Set aside.

3. In another small bowl, combine melted butter, 1 cup warm water and apple cider vinegar.

4. Add butter mixture to dry mixture while beating slowly. Add 4 eggs, 1 at a time. Then add yeast mixture.

5. Mix with electric mixer about 30 seconds on low speed, then beat on high for 2 minutes.

6. Place mixing bowl in warm spot. Cover with towel and let rise until doubled, then beat again for 3 minutes.

7. Pour into well-sprayed bread pan. Let rise until just slightly above pan. Bake at 350° F for 50 minutes.

8. Remove from pan onto cooling rack.

Mary's Tip: If left to raise too much in pan, it will run over sides when baking.

Cinnamon Swirl Bread

Dry Ingredients:

2 cups White Rice Flour Mix (see page 7)

1 cups sugar

1 tsp. xanthan gum

2 tsp. baking powder

½ tsp. baking soda

1 ½ tsp. cinnamon

Wet ingredients:

¾ cup buttermilk

¼ cup vegetable oil

2 eggs

2 tsp. vanilla extract

Cinnamon filling:

⅓ cup brown sugar

2 tsp. cinnamon

1 Tbsp. butter

Instructions:

1. Preheat oven to 350° F. Mix dry ingredients in large mixing bowl. Mix well.

2. Add wet ingredients. Mix well.

3. In small bowl, combine ingredients for cinnamon filling, using a pastry cutter.

4. Spray 2 small loaf pans with cooking spray. Divide half of the batter between 2 small loaf pans (pour one fourth of the batter in each pan).

5. Pour half of the cinnamon filling in each pan.

6. Divide the remaining half of the batter in two parts and spread each part on the top of the cinnamon filling in each bread pan.

7. Bake at 350° for about 40 minutes, or until toothpick comes out clean.

Zucchini Bread

Dry Ingredients:

3 cups White Rice Flour Mix (see recipe page 7)

2 cups sugar

1 ½ tsp. xanthan gum

1 tsp. salt

1 ½ tsp. baking soda

1 ½ tsp. baking powder

2 Tbsp. cinnamon

Wet ingredients:

4 eggs

4 cups fresh shredded zucchini

⅔ cup oil

2 tsp. vanilla

Instructions:

1. In large mixing bowl combine dry ingredients and mix well.

2. Add eggs and blend with mixer on medium until smooth.

3. Add rest of the wet ingredients and blend with mixer.

4. Pour into well-greased bread pans (2 large pans or 3 small pans).

5. Bake for 50 minutes at 350°, or until toothpick comes out clean.

Variations:

Add 1 cup of chopped walnuts, cranberries or a combination of the two.

Recipe can also be used to make 24 muffins.

Banana Bread

Mary's Tip: This makes good muffins and for a variation, you can also add chocolate chips, or cranberries.

Dry Ingredients:

2 cups brown rice flour

⅔ cup sugar

1 tsp. baking soda

¾ tsp. xanthan gum

¼ tsp. salt

1 Tbsp. baking powder

1 tsp. cinnamon (optional)

½ cup chopped walnuts (optional)

Wet Ingredients:

2 – 3 medium, ripe bananas

2 eggs

½ cup vegetable oil

½ cup milk

Instructions:

1. Preheat oven to 350° F. Mix dry ingredients in large mixing bowl. Mix well.

2. Add wet ingredients. Mix until well combined, but do not over beat.

3. Pour batter into sprayed bread pans. Bake 35-45 minutes at 350° F, or until toothpick comes out clean.

4. Cool on rack before wrapping for storage.

Pumpkin Bread

Mary's Tip: This recipe can also be made into muffins and as a variation, you can add chopped nuts.

Dry Ingredients:

1 ¾ cups brown rice flour

1 cup sugar

1 tsp. baking soda

¾ tsp. xanthan gum

¾ tsp. salt

½ Tbsp. baking powder

½ tsp. cinnamon

½ tsp. nutmeg

¾ tsp. pumpkin pie spice

Wet Ingredients:

2 eggs

¼ cup water

⅓ cup + 2 Tbsp. vegetable oil

2 Tbsp. molasses

1 cup pumpkin

Instructions:

1. Preheat oven to 350° F. Mix dry ingredients in large mixing bowl. Mix well.

2. Add wet ingredients. Mix well, but do not over beat.

3. Pour batter into sprayed bread pans. Bake 35-45 minutes at 350° F, or until toothpick comes out clean.

4. Cool on rack before wrapping for storage.

Chocolate Chip Coffee Cake

Ingredients:

2 cups Brown Rice Flour Mix (see page 7)

¾ tsp. xanthan gum

1 ½ tsp. baking powder

1 tsp. baking soda

½ tsp. salt

1 cup sugar

⅓ cup vegetable oil

1 cup sour cream

2 large eggs

2 tsp. vanilla extract

1 cup chocolate chips

Instructions:

1. Preheat oven to 350° F. Spray 9x9 square pan with cooking spray.

2. Mix dry ingredients into mixing bowl until blended. Add eggs, vanilla extract, sour cream and vegetable oil.

3. Mix well. Add chocolate chips and pour batter into a well sprayed pan.

4. Bake about 40 minutes at 350° F, or until toothpick comes out clean.

Cinnamon Rolls

Wet Ingredients:

⅔ cup milk, warmed

1 Tbsp. yeast

2 tsp. butter

¼ cup sugar

1 egg

¼ cup vegetable oil

1 tsp. vanilla

Dry ingredients:

¼ cup potato starch

¾ cup cornstarch

½ cup brown rice flour

¼ tsp. baking soda

2 ½ tsp. xanthan gum

2 tsp. baking powder

½ tsp. salt

Cinnamon filling:

1 cup brown sugar   ⅓ cup butter

2 tsp. cinnamon

Icing:

½ stick butter (¼ cup), softened

8 oz. cream cheese

1 ½ cups powdered sugar

1 tsp. vanilla extract

Instructions:

1. Mix warm milk and yeast in small bowl. Set aside.

2. In large mixing bowl, cream together butter, sugar, egg and oil with electric mixer.

3. In medium mixing bowl, mix together dry ingredients. Add dry ingredients to butter mixture. Blend well.

4. Roll out on well-floured surface in a rectangle. Spread ¼ cup melted butter evenly over dough.

5. In small mixing bowl, mix together the cinnamon filling. Spread evenly over the dough. Roll into a log.

6. Cut rolls about 1 inch wide and place on greased cookie sheet. Allow to rise for 40 minutes.

7. Bake at 350° for 15 minutes, until slightly browned. Do not over bake.

8. Mix icing ingredients using electric mixer. Spread over warm rolls.

Sour Cream Coffee Cake

Ingredients:

2 cup Brown Rice Flour Mix (see page 7)

¾ tsp. xanthan gum

1 ½ tsp. baking powder

1 tsp. baking soda

½ tsp. salt

1 cup sugar

⅓ cup vegetable oil

2 large eggs

2 tsp. vanilla extract

1 cup sour cream

Brown sugar center:

⅓ cup brown sugar

¼ cup butter

2 tsp. cinnamon

⅓ cup pecans

Instructions:

1. Preheat oven to 350° F. Spray 9x9 square pan with cooking spray.

2. Mix dry ingredients into mixing bowl until blended. Add eggs, vanilla extract, sour cream and vegetable oil.

3. Mix well. Pour half of the batter into pan.

4. In small bowl, blend ingredients for brown sugar center. Reserve -3 Tbsp. sugar mix in a small bowl. Spread the rest of the mix evenly on batter.

5. Spread the rest of the batter on top of the brown sugar mix. Sprinkle remaining mix on top.

6. Bake about 40 minutes at 350° F, or until toothpick comes out clean.

Main Dishes & Soups

"I live on good soup, not on fine words."
- Moliere

"Only the pure of heart can make good soup"
- Beethoven

"Beautiful soup, so rich and green
Waiting in a hot tureen!
Who for such dainties would not stoop?
Soup of the evening, beautiful soup!
Beautiful soup! Who cares for fish
Game, or any other dish?
Who would not give all else for two
Pennyworth of beautiful soup?"
- Lewis Carroll, 'Alice in Wonderland'

Coffee House Chili

Ingredients:

1 ½ lbs. ground beef

1 large onion, chopped

1 can (46 oz.) pure tomato juice

1 can (29 oz.) pureed tomato

2 small cans of kidney beans

2 Tbsp. chili powder

½ tsp. black pepper

1 tsp. oregano

1 tsp. cumin

1 tsp. garlic powder

1 tsp. salt

Instructions:

1. Brown ground beef with chopped onion in skillet, crumble, and drain well.

2. Combine browned, crumbled beef with all other ingredients in large stock pot.

3. On medium-high heat, boil for about 20 minutes.

4. Serve hot with corn chips (check label for pure ingredients), shredded cheese, and sour cream.

Mary's Tip: To add some heat to the chili, add chili peppers, chili beans, hot sauce, or any other spicy ingredient of your choice.

Beef & Noodle Soup

Ingredients:

22 cups beef stock

1 can (28 oz.) shredded beef

Salt and pepper to taste

1 ½ cups carrots, chopped

1 ½ cups celery, chopped

1 lb. + 8 oz. Gluten-Free Homemade Noodles (see recipe on page 10)

Instructions:

1. In large stock pan, bring beef stock to a boil.

2. Add salt and pepper to taste, carrots, and celery. Boil until soft.

3. Add noodles. Boil uncovered until noodles are done (approximately 15 minutes). Tip: Do not overcook, noodles will become too soft.

4. Ready to serve. This recipe makes a large quantity and serves 15-20 people.

Vegetable Beef Soup

Ingredients:

2 large jars of tomato juice

2 cups chopped cabbage

1 large onion, chopped

1 large can (28 oz.) cooked beef

1 large bag frozen, mixed vegetables

6 medium potatoes, cubed

1 tsp. garlic powder

½ tsp. pepper

1 tsp. basil

1 tsp. oregano

Instructions:

1. Bring the tomato juice to a boil. Add the cabbage and onion. Boil for 15 minutes.

2. Add the rest of the ingredients. Boil until cabbage is tender. Serve.

Chicken and Noodle Soup

Ingredients:

22 cups chicken stock

1 ½ cup carrots

1 ¼ cup celery

3 cups shredded, cooked chicken

¼ cup browned butter

Salt and pepper to taste

1 lb. & 8 oz. Gluten-Free Homemade Noodles (see recipe page 10)

Instructions:

1. To brown the butter, heat in a skillet over medium heat. Whisk frequently. Heat until butter is a caramel color and quickly remove from heat to avoid burning.

2. Bring chicken stock to a boil.

3. Add carrots, celery, chicken, butter and salt and pepper. Boil until carrots and celery are soft, approximately 30 minutes

4. Add noodles. Boil uncovered until noodles are done, approximately 15 minutes. Tip: Do not overcook, noodles will become too soft.

5. This recipe makes a large quantity and serves 15-20 people.

Sweet and Sour Meatballs

Sweet and Sour Sauce Ingredients:

1 - 20 oz. can pineapple chunks

½ cup brown sugar

⅓ cup water

3 Tbsp. cornstarch

3 tsp. vinegar

1 large green pepper

1 Tbsp. soy sauce

Meatball Ingredients:

1 lb. lean ground beef

1/4 cup minced onion

1 egg

1/2 tsp. salt

2 Tbsp. water

1/8 tsp. pepper

½ cup Gluten-Free Bread Crumbs (see recipe page 9)

Instructions:

1. To prepare meatballs, combine meatball ingredients in large bowl. Form into meatballs about 1 inch in diameter. Bake at 350° for 25-30 minutes, until meatballs are no longer pink in the middle.

2. Drain pineapple and save juice. Add enough water to the pineapple juice to measure 1 cup.

3. Pour liquid into large skillet and add the ⅓ cup water, vinegar, soy sauce, brown sugar, and cornstarch. Use whisk to stir until smooth.

4. Cook liquid over medium heat until thick, stirring constantly.

5. Thinly slice the green pepper. Add pineapple, meatballs and green pepper. Reduce heat and simmer uncovered for 20 minutes.

6. Serve over cooked rice.

Sweet Potato Pudding

Ingredients:

1 medium can sweet potatoes

½ cup milk

¾ cup sugar

2 eggs

⅓ cup butter

½ tsp. nutmeg

½ tsp. cinnamon

Topping:

⅓ cup butter, melted

¾ cup cornflakes (gluten-free)

½ cup chopped pecans

½ cup brown sugar

Instructions:

1. Place sweet potatoes into large bowl and blend with beaters on medium speed until smooth.

2. Add milk, sugar, eggs, butter, nutmeg and cinnamon. Blend of medium speed for about 1 minute.

3. Spread mix into greased 9 inch pie place.

4. Bake at 400° for 20 minutes, or until set.

5. Stir together the topping ingredients, and sprinkle on top of the potatoes, while hot. Bake another 10 minutes.

6. Pour all ingredients into a bowl and mix for 15 seconds. Serve warm.

Chicken Broccoli Casserole

Jennifer's Tip: Even picky eaters (like my kids) love this dish, and it's so easy to put everything together the night before, put it in the fridge, then throw in the oven after work.

Ingredients:

2 bunches chopped broccoli (or frozen)

4-6 boneless chicken breasts – cooked and cut into bite-sized pieces

1 cup Velveeta cheese cut in small cubes (or slices)

1 ½ cups Gluten-Free Cream of Mushroom Soup (see page 8)

½ cup mayonnaise

Pepper to taste

Gluten-Free fried onions

Instructions:

1. Steam the chopped broccoli until crisp tender.

2. In a greased 9x13 pan, layer the broccoli, then the cooked chicken, then the Velveeta cheese.

3. In medium bowl, whisk together the cream of mushroom soup, mayonnaise and pepper. Spread over the top of the Velveeta cheese in an even layer.

4. Bake at 350 for 55 minutes, uncovered.

5. Remove from oven and cover with French Fried onions. Return to oven for 5 more minutes.

6. Remove from oven and let rest for 5 minutes, then serve.

Stuffed Green Peppers

Jennifer's Tip: This recipe comes from my brother-in-law, Scott. He made this while babysitting the kids one summer with green peppers from his garden, and it quickly turned into a family favorite.

Ingredients:

2 large green peppers

¾ lb. ground beef

⅓ cup chopped onion

1 small jar of stewed tomatoes, cut up

⅓ cup long grain rice

1 Tbsp. Worcestershire sauce (check for a gluten-free brand)

½ tsp. basil

½ cup shredded cheddar cheese

½ cup water

¼ tsp. pepper

Instructions:

1. Halve the green peppers lengthwise and remove ends and stems.

2. Bring about 6 cups of water to boil (enough to cover the pepper halves). Place pepper in boiling water and boil for about 3 minutes. (Or, microwave covered for 2 minutes per pepper).

3. Remove from water. Sprinkle the inside of the peppers with salt. Invert on paper towels to drain water.

4. In large non-stick skillet, cook ground beef and onions on medium heat until meat is browned and onions are tender. Drain fat.

5. Stir in tomatoes, uncooked rice, Worcestershire sauce, basil, water and pepper. Bring to a boil, then reduce heat to medium-low, cover, and simmer for 15-20 minutes, or until rice is tender.

6. Stir ¼ cup of cheese into rice mixture. Fill peppers with rice mixture and place filled peppers in glass baking dish.

7. Bake at 375° for 15-20 minutes, until heated through.

8. Remove from oven and sprinkle with remaining cheese. Let stand for 1-2 minutes until cheese is melted. Serve.

Family-Friendly Meatloaf

Ingredients:

1 lb. ground beef

2 eggs

½ cup Gluten-Free Bread Crumbs (see recipe page 9)

½ cup chopped onion

¼ cup ketchup or your favorite gluten-free barbeque sauce

½ tsp. salt

¼ tsp. pepper

Instructions:

1. In large mixing bowl, mix beef, eggs, bread crumbs and onion. Combine well.

2. Form into a loaf shape and set into a greased bread pan.

3. On top of the loaf, make an indent the length of the loaf with the side of your hand. Fill indent with ketchup or barbeque sauce.

4. Bake for 40-50 minutes at 350°.

Mary's Tip: Season to your own taste by adding your favorite seasonings such as chopped bell peppers, mushrooms, seasoning salt, or minced garlic.

Sweet Potato Casserole

Ingredients:

7-8 sweet potatoes

¼ cup half/ half

1/3 cup melted butter

½ cup sugar

1 tsp. vanilla

2 eggs

½ tsp. salt

Topping:

1/3 cup softened butter

1/3 cup brown sugar

1 cup finely chopped pecans

Instructions:

1. Preheat oven 350°.

2. Peel and halve sweet potatoes. Boil in water for 15 minutes until soft.

3. Mix sweet potatoes and half/half with mixer on medium until mashed.

4. Add remaining ingredients and mix well.

5. Pour into greased casserole dish.

6. For topping, use fork or pastry cutter to cut butter and brown sugar into crumbles.

7. Stir in pecans. Sprinkle over the top of the mixture.

8. Bake at 350° for 30 minutes.

Jennifer's Tip: This is a crowd pleaser at holidays! We took a classic recipe and made a few modifications to make it gluten-free.

Chicken Nuggets

Jennifer's Tip: Easy and quick to make in a pinch, and a kid favorite. A healthy alternative to frozen varieties.

Ingredients:

3 Tbsp. butter, melted

2 tsp. Worcestershire sauce

2 large chicken breasts, or 4 chicken breast halves, uncooked

¼ cup Parmesan cheese, grated

½ cup Gluten-Free Bread Crumbs (see recipe page 9)

½ tsp. garlic powder (or to taste)

½ tsp. salt (or to taste)

Instructions:

1. Preheat oven 450°.

2. Cut chicken into bit sized pieces.

3. In a medium-sized bowl, stir together the melted butter and Worcestershire sauce.

4. On a plate, mix Parmesan cheese, gluten-free bread crumbs, garlic powder and salt.

5. Dip chicken into butter mix, then roll in bread crumb mixture. Spread out on a cookie sheet or jelly roll pan.

6. Bake at 450° for 9-10 minutes or until no longer pink.

Pizza Crust

Ingredients:

1 Tbsp. yeast

1 cup warm water

1 tsp. salt

2 Tbsp. vegetable oil

2 cups White Rice Flour Mix (see recipe page 7)

¼ cup powdered milk

1 tsp. xanthan gum

Instructions:

1. Preheat oven to 450° F. Combine yeast and warm water in mixing bowl. Let set 3-4 minutes.

2. Add the rest of the ingredients. Mix until it forms a ball. If too wet, add small amounts of flour until dough is manageable.

3. Divide into 3 balls and roll each out into a circle.

4. Pre-bake each circle on cookie sheet at 450° F for about 10 minutes.

5. Remove from oven, add toppings, and bake until cheese is brown and bubbly

Mary's Tip: If you want to store crusts for future use, pre-bake, then cool. When cool, wrap in plastic wrap individually and freeze. Remove from freezer when needed, and let thaw.

Index

Recipe photographs taken by Stephanie Fisher.

Content edited by Jennifer Brogee and Ruth Ann Stover.

Cover photographs by Stephanie Fisher.

Cover design by Jennifer Brogee.

Made in the USA
Charleston, SC
26 September 2013